YOU OPENED THE DOOR, BUT YOU DID NOT LET HIM IN

(LET HIM IN)

by

LOUIS CAMON

www.tmlcministry.com
louis@tmlcministry.com
229-300-5814

Order this book online at www.trafford.com
or email orders@trafford.com

Most Trafford titles are also available at major online book retailers.

Printed in the United States of America.

ISBN: 978-1-4269-4789-6 (sc)
ISBN: 978-1-4269-4790-2 (e)

Trafford rev. 11/23/2010

 www.trafford.com

North America & international
toll-free: 1 888 232 4444 (USA & Canada)
phone: 250 383 6864 ♦ fax: 812 355 4082

Dedication

This book is dedicated to God's creation "all humanity"
from the beginning to the end of this world.

Acknowledgements

First, I give thanks to God who is the head of my life. It is a pleasure to give thanks to all my family, friends, and loved ones who inspired me to write this book. I would like to give special honor to my parents. My father, Jr. Bishop L.J. Camon, who is gone home to be with the Lord; but, the Word of God he taught me is still in my heart today. He taught me to love in spite of, be on time for God and he will be on time for you, if you stumble, get up and try again, do your best and then try to do a little better. Those are some of the things he taught me that I remember clearly till this day. Some of his favorite scriptures were St. Matthew 1:21; Acts 1:8; Acts 2:1-2; and St. Matthew 1:28-30. My mother, Pastor Madine Camon, trained me up from a baby to do God's will. She continues to encourage me to hold on to God's unchanging hands. She has love and patience for everyone she encounters and she does it with the joy of the Lord. One of her favorite sayings is "This is a beautiful day isn't it," and when you answer "yes" her response is "for the Lord to come." To my sisters and brothers, Ladine, Freddie, Linda, Lynette, and Carl, along with other family members have been a great help to me. Last, but not least, I give thanks to my wife, Janice, and our children Louis III, Laquita, and Jermaine. Also, my grandson, Amari, he brings so mush happiness to my life. They have been there with me in the midnight hour when no one else is around. I would love to call out the names of all the saints and friends who helped and inspired me to write this book, but I would have to write a separate book to tell you how God has bless me through them. Just to name a few, Bishop H.J. Echols and all the Leaders of the First Born Church of the Living God, Dr. Earl Roberts, Dr. Jerry Farwell, Dr. Billy Graham, Dr. Charles Stanley, Dr. Evans, Bishop G.E. Patterson, Bishop T.D. Jakes, and all our locate and community preachers small and great have been an inspiration to me.

Contents

Introduction

The writing of this book is reality and a warning for all human beings. We all have a soul to be saved from destruction. It starts from God the Father drawing us to his son, Jesus, who brings us salvation through the Holy Ghost. God deals with the heart. It makes no difference what condition you are in; he put it in the hearts of man to do his will. Sometimes people have to be reminded why we are here on earth. It is to serve God in spirit and in truth with a clean heart. To the ones who have accepted him, we must be a witness to the rest of the world and let them know God loves them.

CHAPTER 1

GOD DRAWS YOU WITH HIS LOVE
FROM ABOVE

One thing we should keep in our minds is that all of us have a chance to experience God's power, love, and mercy. It makes no difference what race, nationality, or culture you are associated with. Romans 2:11 lets us know that there is no respect of *persons* with God. To receive this love God has for us, we must believe and trust in him through faith. Our only hope is God. He sits high and looks low and he deals with our hearts though faith. Our only hope is God. He sits high and looks low. He deals with our hearts though the Spirit. He will contact you in some manner before you leave this earth and it makes no difference who you are.

The scripture points out in Titus 2:11, *for the grace of God that bringeth salvation, appeared to all men.* The first thing we should say when God draws us is "Yes Lord I accept you in my life." I am reminded of the old hymn that goes *Father, I stretch my hands to thee no other help I know. If thou withdrew thyself from me how whether shall I go?* It is important that we realize God is in control of the whole world and without him, we are nothing. God knows who we are, for he created our spirit and made us from the dust of the earth. He has fashioned us by providing our minds with understanding to do his will. He made the awesome creation of this world to get out attention. Everyone in this world perhaps feel that there is a greater power. Romans 1:20 reads, *For the invisible things of him from the creation of the world are clearly seen, being understood by the things that are made even his eternal power and Godhead so that they are without excuse.* This is where we as Christians share the Word of God, The Good News, and The Gospel to the lost. We are to help enlighten those who have not yet accepted the touch of God.

We realize God does not need any help; however, he chose us to be servants in his kingdom. God is loving and merciful and without him the whole world would be lost. His only begotten son suffered and died because of our sins, and he still draws us to him. There is no greater love than the love God has for us. He witnessed his only begotten son go through misery for 33 years. People were out to destroy his legacy. Jesus was only on the earth one day when the people tried to plan a way to murder him. It was in the minds and hearts of people to destroy Jesus and what he had been sent on earth to accomplish. His son was made sin for us and that caused a separation from his father for a period of time. This was done so that the father would be able to draw us closer to him, and give us another chance to live. It is up to you to accept him in your life.

St. John 3:16 reads, *For God so loved the world, that he gave his only begotten son that who so ever believeth in him shall not perish, but have everlasting life.* There is no excuse in not hearing God's call. He deals directly with the heart of every human being. The deaf, dumb, blind, and even the unbeliever and unlearned knows God is present. Some tend to assume they are on their own and can pick God up and put him down whenever they want to; however, the scripture says in Romans 2:4, *Or despises thou the riches of his goodness and forbearance and longsuffering; not knowing that the goodness of God leadeth thee to repentance.*

Essential Perspectives

- ➢ Sometimes God draws you through the Eye. You may see a message from him without realizing it. You may happen to read something in the Bible or see something elsewhere that catches your attention. Messages can be hidden in everyday things such as: pictures, postcards, flyers, television, internet, or any other method that may catch your eye throughout the day.
- ➢ Sometimes God draws you through the Ear. You may hear the Word of God through preachers, teachers, other Christians, or anyone that is speaking at that particular moment. You could also hear about God on the radio, internet, television, or any other mode of communication.

➢ Sometimes God draws you through the Heart. If a person can not see or hear, God has the power to talk to them and draw them straight from their heart. Everyone has a chance to receive Christ in their life. He knows how to get the message across to all his creation.

➢ Sometimes God draws you through the way people treat you. It may be through a sense of touch, feeling, deeds, or words.

➢ Sometimes, God draws you through the miracles he performs on a daily basis.

➢ Sometimes, God draws you though an experience like Saul when he was converted to Paul.

➢ Sometimes, God draws you by letting you walk by someone who is sharing the Gospel.

Sadly, there are so many people that will not accept God in their lives. They do not want to accept the Word. In St. John 6:44 Jesus said, *No man cometh unto me, except the Father draw him, and I will raise him up at the last day.* God does so much to draw us towards him. He watched the persecution of his only begotten son while he was being spit on, lied on, and whipped all night long. Some say that he was beat beyond recognition. Just imagine our savior hanging on the cross just to save an unjust world of sinners. We caused his suffering and death though our past, present, and future sins. God loves his son, but the scripture points out in Romans 8:22, *he spared not his own son, but delivered him up for us all; how shall he not with him freely give us all things.*

In spite of all we have done and the trouble we have caused, he still draws us with his love. It is sad to know that many times we let Jesus down. We even forget about the love and mercy he has shown us. My advice for you is to give God an opportunity to work in your heart and place your name in the Book of Life. No man knows the day or hour of his return. We are also unaware of how much time we have to live earth. You cannot take a chance by playing with God over and over again. This is a serious matter because it deals with where you will spend eternity. Your soul could be lost forever. The enemy is here to keep you from God long enough to destroy you.

Hebrews 3:7 lets us know, *wherefore as the Holy Ghost said, today if ye will hear his voice, harden not your hearts as in the provocation, in the day of temptation in the wilderness.* God is too powerful to play with. I advise you to study and learn more about him.

GOD

1.1

God is in control of the entire universe because he holds the world in his hands. David said in Psalm 24:1-2, 1) *The earth is the Lord's and the fullness thereof; the world, and they that dwell therein. 2) For he hath founded it upon the seas, and established it upon the floods.*

It may seem as if everything is falling apart, and there is nowhere to turn; however, this is a trick of the devil. The devil is the enemy and a long time adversary of God. He makes you think that he can be a greater and stronger leader than God can. The following question has come up many times: If God is so loving, why didn't he deliver his son, Jesus, from being spit on, having a crown of thrones put around his head, having nails put in his hands and feet, being pierced in his side with blood and water coming out, and finally dying on the cross? They also used the scriptures where Jesus asked God a question in Psalm 22:1 and St. Mark 15:34, *My God, my God, why hast thou forsaken me?* In Hebrew he said, *Eli, Eli lama sabachthani?* The more you read your Bible, the more you will begin to understand what really happened in this situation. God gave his son Jesus to take your place for the sins of the world. Jesus stood before God as sin and he suffered a spiritual death for us. Death was the only price that could be compensated for the sins of the world. Nothing could take the place of the Son of God giving his life. No animal, man, woman, boy, girl, or angel could take the place of Jesus dying on the cross. Through this atonement of Jesus' death, we are able to connect to God again. God did it all for you and me, and for this we should praise him with our whole heart, mind, body and soul everyday of our lives. He has done great and marvelous things form the beginning of times, and he will continue to do great things until the end of times.

We should long for God's love. His love is a part of each and every one of us. This feeling is on the inside of every individual. God's love is the only thing to fill this longing and emptiness we sense. He has given us hope through his son, Jesus. God is our refuge and strength. He carries us though all our troubles and trials we may face. He is our aid before we get in trouble, while we are in trouble, and even when we get out of trouble. What a mighty and loving God we serve?

In order to really appreciate his love, we have to look back over our lives and remember all the things he has done for us. He provides us with spiritual gifts and gifts though nature, by providing our bodies with the things we need to survive. He also gives us a powerful weapon we can use anytime, and that weapon is prayer. If we use this weapon, we will get positive results. God has so many great things for us and all we have to do is claim it through the name of Jesus Christ. God promises us so much. If we live for him, he will honor everything he promises us. The half of what he has in store for everyone has never been told. Who would not serve a God like this?

God questions us at different times in our lives. We sometimes get besides ourselves, and think we have all the answers. We may think we know all the answers from the beginning to the end. Job 38:1 reads *1) Who is this that darkened counsel by words without knowledge?* This lets us know that without God, we do not have any knowledge and it does not make any difference who we are. There are some people who put themselves in high positions, but God lets us know that the last shall be first and the first shall be last. Put God first in everything you do and let him lead the way in your life. We should not only receive God for ourselves, but we should convince sinners to accept the love of God as well. God calls for obedience. All you have to do is hear him. Do not sit down and watch television, listen to the radio, and read the newspaper all day long and forget about God. Give him some of your time. Open up your Bible to see and hear what he has to say to you. God talks to you personally through his Holy Word. If you read his written word, which is the Holy Bible, the Living Word will start popping on the inside of you like popcorn. My mother, Pastor Madine Camon, wrote a song called *I feel like popping up like popcorn for the Lord.* Sooner or later what you put on the inside will begin to show up on the outside.

The devil will try to keep you from reading the Bible because he knows all of God's answers for your life are within it. Hear God's voice and do what he says. God is warning you not to make the same mistake the devil made. Right now, you have a chance to make a difference in your life and be filled with the joy of the Lord. The devil does not have a chance because sin started within him and there is no way for him to get out of it. In contrast, the sin that we have in our heart enters from the outside. Thankfully, God is willing to remove it from your heart at your request. All you have to do is tell the Lord yes and ask him to save you now.

GOD'S LOVE

1.2

God is love and he knows how to love us. He shows his love time after time. He has never stopped loving us and never will. God has a perfect love that is authentic and everlasting. Every person who listens and obeys his commands will be a part of his love. We only have to let him in our heart. God's love is so powerful that it goes beyond what the human eye can see, what the ear can hear, and what the hands can touch. His love sinks deep in the heart. If you let him in, no man can ever take this love away from you. God's love is so powerful that he gets your attention when he passes by.

The devil tries to keep you in darkness and from feeling this love God has for you. He knows that if you feel God's love and let him in your heart, he has lost another soul to the creator of the universe.

We have a conscience that makes us feel guilty when we reject God's Word. The book of Genesis speaks of the conscience of Adam and Eve when they hid themselves from God in the Garden of Eden. It made no difference what they had done because they could still hear God's voice in the cool of the day. God hates sin, but he loves us. He deals with us through the things we see and feel deep down on the inside of our souls. No man can get away from the great salvation God offers through his son, Jesus. The omnipresence of God lets us know that he is present in every situation and place. The scripture informs us that there no place you can hide from God. Psalm 139:7, 8 says to us that 1) *Whither shall I go from thy spirit? Or whither shall I flee from thy presence? 2) If I ascend up into heaven, thou are there: If I make my bed in hell, behold, thou are there.*

All creation recognizes there is a higher power. When we look up towards the sky, we can observe the moon, sun, stars, and changing of the seasons. Man must know that it is a plan by God, the Supreme Being. His presence can be felt on the inside of all humanity. God never changes. He offers his love to everyone and gives it to all that trust and believe in him.

It is very important to know that God deals with us through the spirit. We should not let our fleshly minds take control; conversely, we should listen to God when he speaks. If you open up your hearts to him, this will be the greatest experience you will ever go through. Connect your spirit to the Almighty God.

GOD'S LOVE

1.3

God knows that many individuals will follow down the wrong road and become lost to the power of the enemy. The omniscience of God shows us that he knows everything about this entire world. He knows the past, present, and future. He is patient. Even though he is rejected time and time again, he sets before us a way to escape from sin and destruction. God wants you to come closer and closer to him and become saved by his precious grace. He has the power to make you do what is right and wants you to come to him simply because you love him.

The omnipotence of God shows that he has all power. He can do anything but sin. He is a righteous, Holy God. My advice to you is to do the right things and give God full control over your life. Today is the day that the Lord has made. Pick up your Bible and start reading about God's power, presence, knowledge, love, mercy, patience, and wisdom. Once we realize how powerful God is, we will give him the praise everyday of our lives. If we could just open our eyes and see the beauty of God, our lives will be full of thanksgiving. Time passes around God because he is so great. For this reason, it is important that you do not let the devil fool you and do not let this moment pass you by. The devil offers you all, but he does not have anything to give you. God is speaking to your heart in order for you to obtain the real thing.

1.4

The world moves in a fast paste, producing numerous images in our minds. There are various scenes we wish to observe during our lifetime; for that reason, we travel all over the world searching for them. After we have an opportunity to observe these images, there still seems to be a missing link. God is trying to get your attention by showing his great power. He shows you things that only he could have created. We search for the right thing, person, or place to please us. When we find something missing in our lives, we desire more and more to fill that void. There are also certain sounds we hear through various modes of communication. We may hear a sound from the television or radio. We could even hear a sound in the desert, forest, city, or any place. We become curious about these sounds because they grasp our attention continuously. We know deep down on the inside that the sounds contain a deeper meaning.

Many things we see on a daily basis contain both good and bad characteristics. God controls the good and the Holy things, while the devil controls the evil things. God shows you what you can have by doing what is right. In contrast, the devil paints a dead end picture of what you can have by doing things that are wrong. You can feel that there is a division within yourself, but you don't know how to repair it. Truly, there is a separation and it is between the flesh and the spirit. Your flesh constantly tries to keep your spirit in darkness though the powers of the devil; however, God stands in the midst and shines his light of mercy and love through the darkness. His grace gives your spirit a chance to come out of darkness. When you have lived in darkness for so long, you don't know what you need because you have endured longsuffering. It has become a part of your daily life until God shows up and changes everything. When God shows his love upon you, you will begin to see things that you never noticed before. There is a great and pleasant feeling that comes upon you and it is in your reach. In order to reach it, all you have to do is grasp it with your whole body, mind, heart, and soul. This feeling comes from God, the Father, to all his children because he loves us so much. He gives us an opportunity to have everything we want, need, and desire.

1.5

There are troubles and trials you will have to face after you give your life to God; however, this is only because of the sin the devil brought into the world. The difference now is that you are connected to God again through the awakening of your spirit by the power of God. When your spirit is awakened and saved from sin, you should not mind going through the fire because you will come out as pure gold. Since God has released you from the chains of sin, you can see the light in view. You should not mind going through some trouble and trials at times because you need to know that you are blessed in this life on earth, and the world to come.

The devil will not give up on you. He will try to take away the peace and joy you will contain once you are free. It is a great feeling and the devil does not want you to experience God's love. The devil will try to convince you that this world is your eternal home. He will try to blind you from the evil things he sets upon you. You always have to remember that this is not your home. We are just passing through on our way to where we will spend eternity. In order to go to heaven, you must allow God to use you as his Holy vessel.

LET GOD USE YOU

HAVE YOU FELT GOD'S LOVE PERSONALLY?

EXPLAIN

_____

_____

_____

_____

_____

_____

_____

_____

_____

_____

_____

_____

_____

_____

_____

_____

NOTES

HOW AND WHEN WILL YOU HELP PEOPLE REALIZE GOD IS SPEAKING?

NOW IS THE TIME

_____

_____

_____

_____

_____

_____

_____

_____

_____

_____

_____

_____

_____

_____

_____

_____

_____

NOTES

REMEMBER THE WRITTEN WORD OF GOD HAS POWER

HOW WILL YOU STUDY THE WORD OF GOD AND
BE A EFFECTIVE WITNESS?

_____

_____

_____

_____

_____

_____

_____

_____

_____

_____

_____

_____

_____

_____

_____

_____

CHAPTER 2

You Felt Sorrow For a Moment

Sometimes in our lives, we may feel sorrowful from the things that our family and friends have done to us. They may have inflicted pain upon you in some way. You may have lost some things due to various circumstances that were created by these individuals. You may also feel sorrow due to being away from home. It could also be a result of hunger, sickness, or thirst. Sorrow can also be due to the fact that you don't have all the things you desire. You may be searching for something, but don't know exactly what that something is. You may sometimes lose focus because you desire the things that other people have. They may have more money, a fine house, expensive jewelry, or other nice things. They could even be friends with someone that we wish to be friends with too. When this happens, we lose focus on what is really significant in our own lives.

Many times we feel sorrowful because of the situations we go through. You may think about yourself, rather than what will benefit God and your soul. Many individuals think about the right now and don't focus on their future. Some people get their lives mixed up when they have to deal with sorrow. They think that earthly sorrow is the same as Godly sorrow. They don't think of pleasing God until trouble arise in their lives; however, it is essential to think of pleasing God even before trouble comes. We need to understand that Godly sorrow works repentance unto salvation.

Sometimes we may encounter situations that allow our friends to dictate or guide our every move. In fact, we would rather listen to them instead of the Word of God. We are targeted and preyed upon by people who want to see us fall. Some people do not want to see you up on your feet or traveling in the right direction. The bad thing about this is, if you stay around them long enough, what they do will begin to make sense to you. If you are not careful, then you will fall into the same trap. You will feel as if you do not have anything to repent for. You will forget about what God has done for you and how Jesus died on the cross for your sins. In II Timothy 3:5, the Bible talks about *having a form of godliness, but denying the power thereof: from such turn away.*

2.1

As a result of the fall of Adam and Eve, sin entered into our hearts and we lost everything, until God stepped in. The sinful nature we adopted causes us to change many times in our lives. Nevertheless, God makes provision to lead us in the right direction. We see signs and wonders all over the world, but we have a blind eye and deaf ear that block these things from our reality. We can't see or hear what God is trying to tell us because we allow sin to penetrate into our hearts and minds.

We are not like the angels that sinned because their sin came from the inside. In contrast, our sin came from an outside source. It is important for us not to let the devil change our minds in any situation. Every time you alter from doing the will of God, you take a step backward because you are conforming to the devil's will.

We were made in the likeness of God and have the spiritual ability to connect to our creator. Some follow after the spirit for a little while but ultimately let go. The Godly nature is in all of us, but so is the sinful nature of the flesh. This is why we must let the spirit of God lead and guide us to victory in Jesus Christ. All hope for mankind was lost with the first Adam. Romans 5:12 reads, 12) *Wherefore, as by one man sin entered into the world, and death by sin; and so death, passed upon all men, for all have sinned.*

You must acknowledge Jesus as the second Adam. Romans 5:19-21 reads, 19) *For as by one man's disobedience many were made sinners, so by the obedience of one shall many be made righteous. 20) Moreover the law entered, that the offense might abound. But where sin abounded, grace did much more abound; 21) That as sin hath reigned unto death, even so might grace reign through righteous unto eternal life Jesus Christ our Lord.*

Jesus Christ is able to provide you a permanent connection to God right now and forever. We don't have any excuse for denying or turning our backs on the Lord. We are held accountable for every sinful act we commit. God gets our attention in one way or another. Sometimes, he keeps his hands still and allows the devil to let you feel earthly sorrow which causes you to cry, groan, and moan. This earthly sorrow sometimes causes you to make decisions that you don't really want to keep. At the same time, God intervenes with his grace. Choose grace and stay with God in whatever you do.

2.2

God is not someone to be played with. He is a serious and loving God. You cannot play pity pat with him. Sometimes, he will tolerate those games you play in order to give you a chance to draw closer to true repentance. God wants you to realize that time matters in everything you do. The longer you wait, the more heartaches, troubles, and problems you will encounter in your life. These things will hurt you in the future even when you are delivered from your sins. God has the power to make things light on you if you only do the right things and follow his commands. Sometimes you may take advantage of God's love. You will use him to the very last moment and then try to come to repentance. This is not a good idea because you never know when you are going to take your last breath. No one knows when Jesus will return.

2.3

Sorrow has been expressed and broken down so you can understand the difference between sorrow and true repentance. Sorrow on the outward look is expressed by suffering, mourning, or lamentation. It is the uneasiness of the mind produced by the loss of any good. At some point in time, all of us will encounter suffering throughout our life. In fact, we sometimes deserve to suffer but we do not. Our suffering forces us to reflect on our nature and origin. Real repentance is a door from trouble to harmony. It is caused for you to humble and rid yourself of the pride you have in your life. Stop fantasizing on the things the devil has set before you. Instead, come to the reality of having God in your life. Be real and let the Lord use you. You can start by asking him for forgiveness of your sins and let God know that you are not even worthy to come before him, but only through Jesus Christ, his son. Sorrow implies a sense of loss, guilt, and remorse. Grief is sorrow for no immediate cause. Anguish is sorrow caused by pain, deep disappointment, fruitless longing, or unavailing remorse, ad missed opportunities in life. Whatever situation you are in, just place it in God's hands. If you are not saved, pray to God that he will turn this sorrow into repentance. Believe in him and he will take your situation in his hands and lead you through it. Remember that God made this entire world and he has the power to handle all sorrow. As the song says, there is no sorrow that God can not heal. God looks at you and will not put anymore on you than you can bear. Take advantage of the love God has to offer you.

THIS BOOK DOES NOT HAVE TO BE ABOUT YOU
LET JESUS IN

CHAPTER 2 NOTES

THE SORROW YOU FELT

EXPLAIN

_____

_____

_____

_____

_____

_____

_____

_____

_____

_____

_____

_____

_____

_____

_____

_____

CHAPTER 3

You Opened the Door

The devil may have wrapped you up and taken your strength. The strength you had in the beginning of creation has been taken away from all men after Adam and Eve sinned before the Lord. Man died that very day. The body is very much alive, but his spirit is dead until it is resurrected by God through salvation. The devil does all he can to make sure you keep sleeping and never wake up. Your spirit is dead and the devil does not take any chances of you waking up. He has his demons surrounding you to keep you bound in chains. He makes sure that you are surrounded by darkness so you can't find your way. Even though you are bound, lost, and dead in sin, God gives you strength to open the door to your heart. God has angels watching over you. These Holy Angels keep the devil from killing and destroying you. These angels are strong and mighty. They serve and protect you under the will of God. God took it upon himself to give you the strength to open your door. When you open the door, you will feel God's glory, power, love, and mercy. The scripture explains what happens to some that feel his great power. Hear ye therefore the parable of the sower in St. Matthew 13:19. *19) When any one hearth the word of the kingdom, and understandeth it not, then cometh the wicked one, and catcheth away that which was sown in his heart. This is he which received seed by the way side. 20) But he that received the seed into stony places, the same is he that hearth the word, and anon with joy receivth it. 21) Yet hath he not root in himself, but dureth for a while; for when tribulation or persecution ariseth because of the word, by and by, he is offended. 22) He also that received seed among the thorns is he that hearth the word and the care of this world, and deceitfulness of riches, choke the word, and he becometh unfruitful. 23) But he that received seed into the good ground is he that hearth the word, and understandeth it; which also beareth fruit, and bringeth forth some an hundredfold some sixty, some thirty.*

Some of them were not in it for the right reason, nevertheless God still worked with them, giving each and every one an opportunity to be delivered. At some point in our lives, we all were a wretch undone and once stuck in the muck and marrow clay; however, God showed his power against the ruler of darkness. He came into your heart and gave you enough strength to open your heart to choose everlasting life. God also gave the children of Israel the same opportunity. The children of Israel opened the door to the Lord and he provided them with many blessings. He will not only bless you in heaven, but he will also shower you with blessings while you are living on this earth. It is now time for you to let God go to work in your life since you opened your heart's door to him.

3.1

After going through troubles, heartaches, pains, problems, and sorrows, the Word of God will begin to sound wonderful to you. With the help of God, you opened the door. It was refreshing to your dying soul. Even though you are still in the flesh, you felt your spirit become lifted up higher. Finally, you started leaning and depending on the Lord for his help in everything you carry out. You made up in your mind that this is the life for you. Staying in the midst of saints is very important in this stage of your spiritual growth. They can encourage and help you read and study the Bible, which is the written word of God. As long as you stay in the Word of God, you will be connected to the Living Word. You may not understand what you read now, but if you keep on reading and studying the Bible in its entirety, you will be surprised by the knowledge and wisdom God will grant you. Read and study the Old and New Testaments. Many people have already accepted the Word of God, but they are still challenged by the enemy. This is natural because the enemy wants to destroy your life even more now. As we view people that have experienced this, it may cause us to feel threatened. We should not worry because if we trust in God, he will give us the strength to resist the devil and he will flee from us.

3.2

Jesus showed you through his life and the Word of God from past, present, and future situations, the reasons why you should not close the door in his face. It took the faith of God for you to open the door to him in the first place. Do you remember when there was a time when it was not in your hands or power to open the door? That was a result of you living in darkness and being dead in sin. Now, you may feel as if you have so much power and you don't need anyone else on your side. Those thoughts are the works of the devil. He makes you think that you came through your situation with your own powerful might; however, this is not true. You will soon have to make a final decision to determine how long you will stand there, watch, and wait until you think the time is right. Remember time is running out.

3.3

By opening the door to God's word, you can be transformed and changed into a new person. We can help lead others to opening their hearts doors by planting seeds and watering them. In other words, this is done by spreading the word of God. If you can't meet with people personally, it is a good idea to hand out spiritual flyers, cards, or Bibles to get a hold of their attention. You never know who you may help draw closer to Jesus by doing small things. God's word has power to work on the living and the dead. His word will bring life and it is not like other religions. When you pray while you read the Bible, you can help stir up the spirit within yourself and that will help you build a closer and more personal relationship with God. It is a wonderful feeling when you know God personally. This will really work if you are serious about your soul. Ask God to come into your life. Make sure you listen to the word of God while he is speaking to you through the scriptures. You will see and feel the door of your heart opening for him to come in. The feeling of love, peace, and joy you will embrace will let you know that you are on the right path. Love, peace, and joy are the beginning of the fruits of the spirit. Revelation 3:20 tells us, *Behold, I stand at the door and knock; If any man hear my voice, and open the door, I will come in to him, and will sup with him, and he with me.*

God is all powerful, but he still desires to be close to you and enter your heart. Give God some of your time in a quiet place and dedicate that time to him only. You should take out some time in your busy schedule to talk with Jesus. If you talk, I promise you that he will listen. Don't be afraid to let him in. The devil will try to keep you busy by making you do other unnecessary things to take your mind away from God; however, resist the devil and stay on the right path with God. To open the door is a necessity, especially if you expect to meet Jesus in heaven. God's word always upholds the name of Jesus. God's people should help others reach salvation. Every Christian should bring fellowship to their community. They need to let people know that salvation is free and convenience them to let Jesus in. Through Jesus dying on the cross and rising again on the third day, he is the one who makes it possible for God, the Father, to open our heart's door.

THIS BOOK DOES NOT HAVE TO BE ABOUT YOU
LET JESUS IN

CHAPTER 3 NOTES

YOU OPENED THE DOOR

EXPLAIN

_____

_____

_____

_____

_____

_____

_____

_____

_____

_____

_____

_____

_____

_____

_____

_____

CHAPTER 4

JESUS IS STANDING AT YOUR DOOR

Jesus is standing at the door of your heart and asking for you to let him in. We ask the question, why should we let him in? When we look at our lives, we think it is the way it is supposed to be. According to the traditions of our forefathers, we are taught that life is given to us through a natural birth from or mother's womb. We go through life searching and hoping to find real peace. What we fail to realize is that peace is within our reach at all times. That peace comes from Jesus Christ standing at the door reaching out to us trying to get our attention. He wants you to see him for who he really is. In Revelation, 3:20 it reads, *Behold, I stand at the door and knock; if any man hear my voice, and open the door, I will come into him, and sup with him, and he with me.* The most serious decisions you will ever make in your life are to listen and obey the words of God. Hebrews 2:3-4 reads, 3) *How shall we escape, if we neglect so great salvation; which at the first began to be spoken by the Lord, and was confirmed unto us by them that heard him. 4) God also bearing them witness, both with signs and wonders and with divers miracles, and gifts of the Holy Ghost according to his own will?*

The word of God is also known as the Gospel and it is considered the Good News. The will of God is centered around Jesus. Your life will be turned around for the better if you become concerned about Jesus and what the word of God says. The Bible is the book to read and study in order to find all the answers to the questions of life. The Bible contains sixty-six books in its entirety. This inspirational book is divided into two testaments, the Old and the New. There are thirty-nine books in the Old Testaments and twenty-seven books in the New Testament. The Bible will come alive in your life if you only surrender your thoughts when you read each section. One thing you will find out about the Bible is that it is centered on the teachings of Jesus Christ. When we read our Bibles our minds may wonder in many directions because it is led by the enemy to distract us from understanding the scriptures. The devil wants to keep us in unbelief and in utter darkness. His job is to keep us from seeing Jesus. No matter what tricks the devil tries, the light of Jesus continues to shine through the midst of the storms and chaos. He is a light that sits on a hill that cannot be hidden. Some people may ask, what is this that I feel drawing me in the right direction? It's Jesus dealing with you. It is up to you to accept him into your life.

THIS BOOK DOES NOT HAVE TO BE ABOUT YOU
LET JESUS IN

CHAPTER 4 NOTES

JESUS IS STANDING AT YOUR DOOR

EXPLAIN

_____

_____

_____

_____

_____

_____

_____

_____

_____

_____

_____

_____

_____

_____

CHAPTER 5

THE ENEMY SEES JESUS FROM THE INSIDE

Questions are asked about the enemy on a daily basis. Who is the enemy? Where is the enemy? What is the enemy's goal? When does the enemy come to us? Why should I be concerned about the enemy? How did the enemy get on the inside? Listed above are just a few questions people often inquire about the enemy of God. Since you have read the questions, it may have appeared to you that the enemy is the root cause of all sin and evil. Satan, better known as the devil, is the greatest enemy of God and man. The history of the devil points out that he was created by God as a good angel in heaven. The scriptures indicate in Ezekiel 28:14 &15, 14) *Thou art the anointed cherub that covereth; and I have set these so: thou wast upon the holy mountain of God, thou has walked up and down in the midst of the stones of fire. 15) Thou was perfect in thy ways from the day that thou was created, till iniquity was found in thee.* Satan wanted all the praise for himself. He sinned against God and was thrown out of heaven. He could not do anything with God, so he chose to deceive man in the Garden of Eden. He was successful in persuading Adam and Eve to sin. This is the way he enters into all humanity, through the sins of our earthly parents. The first Adam followed the devil's advice; however, the second Adam, known as Jesus Christ, stood the test and denied the trials of the devil. Through Jesus Christ is now the only way to be delivered from the sins of the devil. Out of all that you have done to deny Jesus, he still stands at your door waiting patiently for you to let him in. He wants to give you a chance to be saved. God now gave you the power to open the door and the devil can look out and see Jesus. St. Matthew 8:29 reads, *And, behold, they cried out, saying, what have we to do with thee, Jesus, thou son of God? Art thou come hither to torment us before the time?*

The devil knows that Jesus is your only hope to defeat him. Satan also has power. He even opposed on the chief angels in the tenth chapter of Daniel. Michael, the archangel, was in contents with the devil and said Lord rebuked thee. Satan is known as the prince of the air (Ephesians 2:2). However, Satan knows his limitations when he sees Jesus. The Bible says that the devil trembles at the name of Jesus. When the devil sees Jesus at your door, he knows it is time for him to leave. The devil hopes to offer you enough of this world to keep you on his side, even though he is not able to give you anything, he sill offers you everything. The devil offers death, but Jesus offers life. In St. John 10:10 it reads, *The thief cometh not, but for to steal, and to kill, and to destroy: I am come that they might have life, and that they might have it more abundantly.* Of all the stealing, killing, and destruction the devil is known for, it cannot stand because he has to flee when he sees Jesus. Jesus' glory and power shines through the door when it opens and the devil cannot stand all of God's goodness. The devil knows Jesus as the Son of God and the King of Kings.

The devil might run, but he will not get very far. He is around the bend waiting to see if you are going to accept Jesus in your life. This is a great time for you to know that God has given you the power to accept him in your life at this very moment. The decision lies in your hands. The enemy had you in chains that kept you bound; however, when they were loosened you felt better because all your burdens were lifted. This is the time when you should begin to thank God for his mercy and love.

The Bible explains how some accept Jesus for just a little while. In St. Matthew 13:18-23, Jesus speaks a parable saying, 18) *Hear ye therefore the parable of the sower. 19) When any one hearth the word of the kingdom, and understandeth it not, then cometh the wicked one, and catcheth away that which was sown in his heart. This is he which received seed by the way side. 20) But he that received the seed in stony places, the same is he that hearth the word, anon with joy receiveth it. 21) Yet hath he not root in himself, but dureth for a while: for when tribulation or persecution ariseth because of the word, by and by he is offended. 22) He also that received seed among the thorns is he that hearth the word; and the care of this world, and the deceitfulness of richess, choke the word, and he becometh unfruitful. 23) But he that received seed into the good ground is he that hearth the word, and understandeth it; which also beareth fruit, and bringeth forth some a hundredfold, some sixty, some thirty.* This passage of scripture lets you know that many need to do more than just see Jesus when the devil leaves you. Jesus comes to abide in your heart and he wants you to give him your soul. Jesus doesn't want you to be only a hearer of the word of God, but also a doer. When some of these people in the parable started feeling better, they forgot all the things that devil put them through. Similarly, in this life when Jesus runs the devil away, we sometimes seem to forget all the pain and suffering the devil caused us. We also forget the power of God that was set forth to run Satan away. We should always be thankful for God and his saving power.

THIS BOOK DOES NOT HAVE TO BE ABOUT YOU
LET JESUS IN

CHAPTER 5 NOTES

THE ENEMY SEES JESUS

EXPLAIN

_____

_____

_____

_____

_____

_____

_____

_____

_____

_____

_____

_____

_____

_____

_____

_____

CHAPTER 6

You Closed the Door in Jesus Face

Oh what a wonderful feeling you experienced when some of your problems were lifted and the chains were loosened from your life. You feel the anointing of the Lord in your life and now you know he is full of love and mercy. He loves you so much that he shows you the way from darkness to light. Everything seems so clear now since you have met the savior. You have heard about Jesus many times in the past. When reading your Bible, you know that he is not an ordinary man. According to St. John 1:1-5, 1) *In the beginning was the Word, and the Word was with God, and the Word was God. 2) The same was in the beginning with God. 3) All things were made by him; and without him was not anything made that was made. 4) In him was life, and the life was the light of men. 5) The light shineth in darkness, and the darkness comprehended it not.*

Jesus is Lord and you should let him in your heart right now. Please don't wait another day. I know the enemy has planted seeds of doubt in our lift. He has you hoping for the wrong things in life. Jesus is ready to come in your life, but for some reason you want him to wait a little while longer. You placed the savior of this world on a waiting list. This may be the last time. We never know when our time will be up. No man knows the moment or the hour of Jesus' return. This delay means that the devil is still in charge of your life. This is one of the devil's tricks to make you say that you are not ready to accept Jesus into your life just yet. Every individual know the things that keep them from letting Jesus in. Others know that following Christ is the only way. Yet, they choose to wait until tomorrow. What is very surprising to some people is that tomorrow may never come. You need to know that when you wait to accept Christ in your life, you are playing a game with the creator. He loves you too much to play games with your life. Many people think the door will continue to be open over and over again. It needs to be understood that Jesus is covering us. You are protected for the moment because Jesus stands there for us and God loves his son so much that he has compassion on us because of Jesus. The Bible tells me that Jesus prayed for us that we will soon come around to him before it is too late. Jesus is still standing at the door while you are deciding whether or not if you want to let him in.

I have come to the conclusion that some people love misery and some love being trapped in the enemy's camp. It is now a part of their everyday life because they are constantly running from the blessings of the Lord. The scripture tells us in Isaiah 55:6, *Seek ye the Lord while he may be found, call ye upon him while he is near.* The prophet of the Old Testament told you over and over again about Jesus before he was even born. According to the scripture in Joel 2:12-13 it reads, *12) Therefore also now, saith the Lord, turn ye even to me with all your heart, and with fasting, and with weeping, and with mourning. 13) And rend your heart, and not your garments, and turn unto the Lord your God; for he is gracious and merciful, slow to anger and of great kindness, and repenteth him of the evil.* Jesus is the only one that can connect us to God the Father in Heaven. He will connect our sinful hands to God's Holy Hands. Jesus passed the test by shedding his blood and taking the sins of the world upon himself. This was not an easy test for the Jesus to pass, but he triumphs over all of his enemies. He rose from the dead and now sits on the right hand of God. He has all authority and power. According to Hebrews 9:24, Jesus is currently standing before God on our behalf. Jesus told us that if we let him in, he would go away and prepare a place for us. All we have to do is trust and believe in him and do whatever he says.

Christ is the head of all things that are right and true. At all costs, you should accept Jesus in your life because he is faithful at his word. The fullness of the Father is in him and you must be born again to have eternal life. So, why do you want to close the door in Jesus' face? Remember this is your only hope to making it to heaven. Don't close the door in your saviors face. God is a Holy God and sin has to be destroyed and you don't have to be a part of sin. There may be times in your life when you feel that you are too bad or evil for the Lord to save you; however, he said in his word that he came to save the sinner. Jesus also said he that rejected and received not my Lords hath one that judged him. The word that I have spoken, the same shall judge him in the last day. Jesus is Holy and he is full of love and mercy, but there is still judgment coming for everyone. Make sure you are on the right road. Don't let the devil fool you and make you close the door in Jesus' face because that will be the biggest mistake you can ever make in your life. There is no excuse for not accepting Jesus into your life. He is begging you now, but there will come a time when the begging and pleading will end. When that happens, it will be time for suffering and pain. In other words, there is no more hope for you. It is in your hands now to avoid this evil.

As I have said before, choose life in Jesus Christ, our savior. Jesus is the Father of the Church and you can not go around him in any way. There are false prophets throughout this world that do not acknowledge Jesus as the Son of God. They think they are pleasing the Father by looking over his son Jesus; however, the Bible says that Jesus is the brightness of God's glory. If you are going to shut the door in his face, that is an insult. The sad thing about it is, he still has the power to open the door, but he chose not to because in times of trouble, you may have said that you didn't want to serve him anyway. If you don't serve him from your heart, in spirit and in truth, he cannot accept you as a member of his church. You have to have a change in your mind and heart. It is an insult to close the door in anyone's face, but if you close the door in the savior's face, then you are automatically throwing away your own life. This is a chance that many people wish they had all over again, but sadly, it's too late for some.

St. Luke 16: 19-24 reads, 19) *There was a certain rich man, which was clothed in purple and fine linen, and fared sumptuously everyday. 20) And there was a certain beggar named Lazarus, which was laid at his gate, full of sores. 21) And desiring to be fed with the crumbs which fell from the rich man's table: moreover the dogs came and licked his sores. 22) And it came to pass, that the beggar died and was carried by the angels into Abraham's bosom: the rich man also died and was buried. 23) And in hell, he lifted up his eyes, being in torments, and seeth Abraham afar off, and Lazarus in his bosom. 24) And he cried and said, Father Abraham, have mercy on me, and send Lazarus that he may dip the tip of his finger in water and cool my tongue; for I am tormented in this flame.* This is just one of the parables Jesus used to describe the dangers of living in sin by not having him in your life.

What amazes me is that the same people who were healed and ate the food Jesus blessed them with, were the same ones who cried out crucify him, crucify him, as he hung on the cross. This is the same way it is today. The ones you give bread and water to are usually the ones who will turn their backs on you. When they do this, keep on showing them love even more than before. They have a soul that needs to be saved and there is a God that does not want anyone to be lost. Even though the people killed Jesus and turned their backs on him, he still instructed his disciples to witness to them. He said in St. Matthew 28:18-20, 18) *And Jesus came and spoke unto them, saying, All power is given unto me in heaven and in earth. 19) Go ye therefore, and teach all nations, baptizing them in the name of the Father, and of the Son, and of the Holy Ghost. 20) Teaching them to observe all things whatsoever I have commanded you; and lo, I am with you always, even unto the end of the world. Amen.*

THIS BOOK DOES NOT HAVE TO BE ABOUT YOU
LET JESUS IN

CHAPTER 6 NOTES

YOU CLOSED THE DOOR IN JESUS' FACE

EXPLAIN

_____

_____

_____

_____

_____

_____

_____

_____

_____

_____

_____

_____

_____

_____

_____

CHAPTER 7

You did not Repent

You deceived yourself with the sorrow you had in your heart because of the things you wanted or lost. As time passed, you were ready to start all over again but you continued walking on the same path. You really think it will be better this time around because that is what the enemy told you. He told you this so you would not give God your heart. Now, it is a waiting process and you are waiting to see if your life will become better, stay the same, or become worse. Sometimes it will take a while for you to start feeling the pressure and it may not occur overnight. Who knows what the outcome will be for you? I really hope it is not too late and you have another chance. There have been questions asked. For example, will God give you up to a reprobate mind to do the things which are not convenient? The Bible tells you more about this in the first chapter in the book of Romans. God has done a lot of wonderful things for you; however, you just can't seem to let the worldly things go. The devil makes you feel like those things are a part of your nature and you cannot live without it. With this temptation, you have experienced the greatest power in the universe. The devil deals with untruths and he paints a picture of the things you will be missing out on, but it all leads to destruction of your spirit, soul, and body.

You once started out in the right direction as a seed that was planted in the ground, but somewhere along the way, you gave up. Even though you may be on the wrong path, you still have great potential to do work for the Lord. God is ready to use you to spread the Good News, or the Gospel of Christ. My advice is that you catch hold to Jesus and never let go. The Bible is a wonderful example for the world to follow. A lack of obedience and unfaithfulness to the Lord can cause many bad things to happen. That is what happened to many people in the Bible. All types of people are in the Bible, but the ones who accepted the Lord were full of joy, peace, and love. Their home is now in heaven. In the book of Isaiah 1:16-19, God speaks to us by saying, 16) *Wash you, make you clean; put away the evil of your doings from before mine eyes; cease to do evil. 17) Learn to do well; seek judgment, relieve the oppressed, judge the fatherless, plead for the widow. 18) Come now, and let us reason together, saith the Lord; though your sins be as scarlet, they shall be as white as snow; though they be red like crimson they shall be as wool. 19) If you be willing and obedient, ye shall eat the good of the land.*

God shows his love to the just, as well as the unjust. He also shows his precious love to the righteous, as well as the unrighteous. Our sins are terrible before the eyes of the Lord because he completely hates sin. It is an unpleasant odor to his nostrils. Jesus is the one who is standing in the gap for you with his arms open wide. Your eyes were open and you saw the light, but you did not acknowledge it and repent. The Lord knows that you draw near to him with your mouth, but your heart is far from him; however, this will not stop the Lord from doing marvelous things in the midst of his people. Sooner or later all the wicked people will be brought to naught and the scorner will be consumed. Those that watch for iniquity will be cut off. Jesus offers you a way of holiness, but the unclean and foolish will pass over it because they overlook God and his righteousness. Isaiah 53:5 reads, *He was wounded for our transgressions, he was bruised for our iniquities; the chastisement of our peace was upon him, and with his stripes, we are healed.*

If you didn't repent yet, what are you trying to do? Are you trying to wait until you get old and worn out before you decide to give your heart to God? He is the one who deserves the honor, praise, and thanks. Ecclesiastes 12:1-2 reads, *Remember now thy Creator in the days of thy youth, while the evil days come not, nor the years draw nigh, when thou shalt say, I have not pleasure in them. 2) While the sun, or the light, or the moon, or the stars, be not darkened, nor the clouds return after the rain.* If you are not careful, you will become set in your ways and you will be lost forever. The strength, beauty, money, riches, and nice things you have can sometimes cause you to have too much pride and you put those things before God Almighty. The earthly possessions do not buy us time, but our time lies within God. I know that I may sound repetitious, but I don't want you to fall short and lose my blessing for not spreading the Gospel to you and the rest of the world. You only have one life to live and I honestly want you to live for Christ.

THIS BOOK DOES NOT HAVE TO BE ABOUT YOU
LET JESUS IN

CHAPTER 7 NOTES

YOU DID NOT REPENT

EXPLAIN

_____

_____

_____

_____

_____

_____

_____

_____

_____

_____

_____

_____

_____

_____

CHAPTER 8

THE ENEMY RETURNS AND FINDS YOUR HOUSE EMPTY

The enemy ran when you opened the door to your heart and let Jesus in. He made you think that he was gone for ever and you would not have any more problems in your life. However, he did not go too far. He is just around the bend peeping and planning his next move. He watches as God shows you love, mercy, and grace and he calls you a fool for believing in God. He laughs at you constantly knowing that if you don't accept Jesus, he will have a chance to afflict you with more suffering, pain, and misery. How can you allow yourself to return back to the bondage of sin, after you have been released from those chains? Please don't let the devil back into your life. He has a few more tricks to attempt in order to try to complete his mission. You were able to get away from Satan the last time because you were begging, crying, fasting, groaning, mourning, and praying to God to be released from the enemy's grip. The mighty hands of God delivered you out of the hands of the enemy by giving you another chance. God proved to you that he has power over the devil by making him leave your house. The enemy had no choice but to let go because God was in your presence. The devil trembles in the midst of God, so how can he make you feel like you are greater than your creator? The enemy has you serving the creature and not the creator of the entire universe. Angels watch over you through the power of God, but they can not keep the enemy from coming into your life. God puts that choice in your hands whenever Jesus comes to you. The enemy's ultimate goal is to take you out by killing, stealing, and destroying you in any way possible. He is wise in his own way.

Ezekil 28: 3- 4 reads, 3) *Behold, thou art wiser than Daniel; There is no secret that they can hide from thee; 4) With thy wisdom and thine understanding thou hast gotten thee riches, and has gotten gold and silver in thy treasure.* You should not want to play with the enemy. He will use any means necessary to defeat you. Sometimes his biggest weapons against you are your own family members, friends, and other enemies. Then he tries to destroy them after he is finished using them to destroy you. He knows that he is never going back to heaven; therefore, he continues putting stumbling blocks in your way to hinder you from going to heaven as well. His method is to have no survivors. My advice to you is to leave the devil outside where he belongs. Let Jesus be your sword and shield of protection. Fill your house with God's presence and glory. The devil is on his way back to you, so you need to accept Jesus in your life now. The enemy has a surprise this time to shake you up from the inside out. He is bringing seven more of his friends with him. St. Matthew 12: 43-45 reads, 43) *When the unclean spirit is gone out of a man, he walketh through dry places, seeking rest, and findeth none. 44) Then he saith, I will return into my house from whence I came; and when he come he findth it empty, swept, and garnished. 45) Then goeth he, and taketh with him seven other spirits more wicked than himself, and they enter again and dwell there, and the last state of that man is worse than the first. Even so shall it be also unto this wicked generation.*

Some people think they cannot live unless they are bound in slavery. They believe this is a part of God's plan. In contrast, God's plan for you is to be full of joy, peace, and love. This reminds me of a story in the Bible when God sent Moses to deliver the children of Israel from the land of Egypt. They were used to the pain and suffering and where somewhat satisfied. God wanted to change their situation, but they were rebellious and fought against their own freedom. Many times they put themselves back into harms way. God delivered them over and over again. They could only see through fleshly eyes and that made it easy for the devil to use them. The devil make things look better by dressing it up.

Now, when the enemy comes back to his home, he starts to work on you all over again along with his seven other friends he brings with him. He gets you tangled up in color barriers, racial fights, lust, dysfunction, superiority, animosity, peer-pressure, trouble, and the list goes on and on. Lust is a major problem. The eyes see and the ears hear, and that causes us to want the things we know we should not have. The enemy uses lust daily to destroy many lives. Some lust over land, cars, diamonds, gold, houses, and material things. Many individuals feel the need to have to have various items at any cost. Some lust over women, men, boys, and girls. They can see that destruction is in sight but they still long for those things.

I am reminded of a true story that an AIDS victim told me about lust. The man said he saw a pretty female and he knew she had full blown AIDS. After watching her for several days, he still decided to have sexual relations with her even though he knew her situation. The enemy worked on him and gave him a plan. The man said one night the enemy told him that if he get drunk and went through with the sexual act then everything would be okay. The man followed through with the instructions given to him by the enemy. The enemy had to be laughing at him. After the man went through with the sexual ordeal, he contracted Aids, then the enemy tried to turn him against God. The devil and demons are enemies of God and man. They will cause you to hurt people you love and even yourself. Look at what's happening all over the world and even in our home towns. Spouses are killing each other, children are killing their parents, parents are killing their children and the list goes on and on.

One of the many reasons this is happening is because the enemy is trying to destroy every single human being. After knowing this information, why would you want to let him back into your life? I do not know. The enemy looks so innocent and tries to get you to trust him. He looks lonely and tries to make you feel sorry for him. The enemy even makes you feel as though you are being mistreated by people around you. Sometimes, the enemy looks very beautiful and as radiant as a shinning star and he uses his beauty to entangle you and your character. Watch out for the enemy because he will devour you, sneak up on you, and demolish you to prevent you from spreading the good news of Jesus Christ. Avoid the enemy to prevent yourself from being snarled in a knot. Your only hope now is to repent and ask God for forgiveness if you have allowed the enemy back into your life. It will work and God will answer all your prayers if only you believe he can do it.

THIS BOOK DOES NOT HAVE TO BE ABOUT YOU
LET JESUS IN

CHAPTER 8 NOTES

THE ENEMY RETURNS AND FINDS YOUR HOUSE EMPTY

_____

_____

_____

_____

_____

_____

_____

_____

_____

_____

_____

_____

_____

_____

_____

_____

CHAPTER 9

JESUS THE HUMBLE LAMB

Jesus is the humble Lamb of God and he still stands at the door that was closed in his face. What other person do you know would do such a thing after he has eased your burdens, pain, and suffering? The truth is people want what they can get from the Lord, but they still want to be free to do as they please. They react upon how they feel at that very moment and it doesn't matter if it's right or wrong. These people were able to smile again, their burdens were lifted, and for a moment they had peace in their hearts because Jesus, the King of Glory, shimmed in their hearts. Look at the results they received by allowing Jesus to shine within them. They allowed God to use them in a mighty way. Jesus, the humble Lamb of God, brings love, joy, and peace with him when he comes to your heart. The love, joy, and peace he brings is everlasting when you let him in your heart's door. No one can take this away from you, not even the devil and his demons. When Jesus comes in your heart, this does not mean you will not have any troubles and trials because you are still in the flesh and the devil will approach you everyday in your life. He will try to steal this special gift away from you; however, it cannot be done because your spirit is sealed until the day Jesus returns to take his people away to be with him in heaven. Sometimes God starts the process over again in your life. Not because of you, but because of his son, Jesus. The humble Lamb of God is standing on behalf of you before his father in heaven. Jesus humbled himself down to a human being to be a part of the human race. He was born in Bethlehem of Judea and lived a life free from sin. Jesus suffered, died, and rose again to save the world from sin. Jesus, the Word of God, was made flesh then he gave up his throne in glory to save the lost sheep. He was obedient to his Father's will. God is love and Jesus is the brightness of his Glory. Out of all the things Jesus has been through for your sake, he still offers a great invitation in St. Matthew 11:28-30 when he says, 28) *Come unto me all ye that labor and are heavy laden, and I will give you rest. 29) Take my yoke upon you, and learn of me; for I am meek and lowly in heart, and ye shall find rest unto your souls. 30) For my yoke is easy, and my burden is light.*

Jesus could have came down from heaven to earth and made a great kingdom with his angles. Conversely, he chose to do the work of his earthly father, Joseph, who was a carpenter. The only way people were able to know Jesus was through the spirit and not the flesh. Jesus came to baptize with the Holy Ghost and fire; however, he allowed John to baptize him in the Jordan River. Jesus took the time to explain parables so that even a little child could feel his love on the inside and show it on the outside.

Jesus' own people, the Jews, did not recognize him as their Lord and Savior. The ones that knew him personally even questioned his leadership. He grew up with the Jews and began to spread the Gospel at an early age. The great leaders were amazed at the wisdom and knowledge of Jesus. In spite of everything, he was rejected; nevertheless, he humbled himself and continued to show love. One thing that men should know is that he will not always toil with them as they continue to sin. It does not matter if you are a man, woman, boy, or a child. He is one hundred percent for holiness and one hundred percent against sin. Some people may change but the Bible lets us know that Jesus is the same yesterday, today, and forever. God gives you time to make things right with your creator and receive him into your heart.

John was chosen to introduce Jesus. No one could have prepared a greater introduction than John. He followed God's instruction by leading the way to repentance through water baptism. John automatically let the world know that he was not the messiah, but he was just presenting him to the world. According to the New Testament, Jesus was introduced as the Word in the first chapter of John. His nature was God and he was an agent in creating the world. The nature of God was holiness and Jesus revealed this to man so they could understand the Father's love. Before this world was formed, Jesus was on the right hand of the Father expressing his love for his followers even before the foundation of the world was laid.

John explained Jesus' identity not only as a man, but as God. He said the Word was with God, and the Word was God. The divinity of Jesus had to be known to the whole world. Everything that was created, visible and invisible, was through Jesus. The whole world depends on him to survive. Jesus gave us life on earth and offers us eternal life in the world to come if we believe in God.

Jesus is different from others; he goes deep into the heart and mind of every believer. If you trust in him, he will be a light to lead you out of darkness. He is not hidden from the world, but he is known through the conscience of every individual. If we listen to him speak to our hearts, he will lead and guide us to do the will of the father. Jesus was right here among us and was not only known as the creator. He was denied by many people as being God. When he was born into the world by the Virgin Mary, he was one hundred percent man. He dealt with all the things humans deal with, but he did not fall to the temptation of sin. He was also one hundred percent God and was filled with love, mercy, kindness, and longsuffering.

Everyone has the right to know him personally because he shed his innocent blood, suffered, died on the cross, and rose again. Jesus knows what you are going through because as a man, he had to bare our burdens and sins on the cross. Jesus lives through people who accept him as their savior He is the Lamb of God because he sacrificed his life for the sins of the world. Jesus is the perfect sacrifice. The father gave us a wonderful gift. He has the power to take away your sins if you simply believe.

THIS BOOK DOES NOT HAVE TO BE ABOUT YOU
LET JESUS IN

CHAPTER 9 NOTES

JESUS THE HUMBLE LAMB

EXPLAIN

_____

_____

_____

_____

_____

_____

_____

_____

_____

_____

_____

_____

_____

_____

_____

_____

CHAPTER 10

JESUS THE ROARING LION

Jesus, the roaring lion, gives everyone a chance to receive him inside their hearts. Some individuals thinks Jesus change, but the Bible points out that he is the same yesterday, today, and forever. He stands firm for the same principles since the beginning of creation. The main point is he is Holy and against all sin and evil. There will come a time when God will tell his son Jesus that it is over. He will continue to tell him, you did everything you could do to help these people, yet some chose to not take heed. You supplied their needs, came down from your heavenly throne, taught them personally, suffered persecution, was spit on, beat all night long, killed, and crucified. All these things happened to you, but yet and still you said Father forgive them for they know not what they do. Then you were raised from the dead, preached salvation, and many still refused to invite you into their hearts.

Jesus rose from the grave and went back to heaven and made a connection with God, the father. There is no other way to get to God, except through Jesus. There are religious groups that deny Jesus as being Lord. The Bible explains in specific details who Jesus is and his purpose in our lives. The signs of time warns every man, woman, boy, and girl that the end is almost near. Just take a look at the conditions of the weather. Sometimes it is hot in the winter and cold in the summer. If you are not saved, this should grasp your attention. We should not only look at the weather's conditions, but also the fact that God is love. The knowledge we have about the end of times is too valuable to overlook. 1 Thessalonians 5:2 reads, *For yourselves, know perfectly that the day of the Lord so cometh as a thief in the night.* If you are not ready when Jesus comes, you will not have time to say "Lord help me." People invent new things to take the place of God in their lives and often terrible things happen to them and their families. Sadly, repenting is not on their agenda. In fact, it is not even on their minds.

Jesus is obedient to the call of his father. When God tells Jesus "this is it", he will be on his way back for his people. If you are not saved, there is no chance of receiving the Holy Ghost because it will be too late. Some will try to justify what they did and reasons for doing those things that interfered with their walk with Jesus. There will also be some people who started out walking with the Lord, but didn't fully accept him into their hearts. They kept him on alert because they still wanted to sin although they may have claimed to be saved. Jesus knows your heart. In St. Matthew 7:21-23 it reads, 21) *Not everyone that saith unto me, Lord, Lord shall enter into the kingdom of heaven; but he that doeth the will of my father which is in heaven. 22) Many will say to me in that day Lord, Lord have we not prophesied in thy name? and in thy name have cast out devils? and in thy name done many wonderful works? 23) And then will I profess unto them, I never knew you; depart from me, ye that work iniquity.*

It is a terrible thing if the Lord does not know you. The only way to know him is in the spirit. Get to know him personally before you end up in darkness.

THIS BOOK DOES NOT HAVE TO BE ABOUT YOU
LET JESUS IN

CHAPTER 10 NOTES

JESUS THE ROARING LION

EXPLAIN

_____

_____

_____

_____

_____

_____

_____

_____

_____

_____

_____

_____

_____

_____

_____

CHAPTER 11

The Holy Ghost

The Holy Ghost is the spirit that moves and works through faith. The Holy Ghost is also God. There is God the Father, God the Son, and God the Holy Ghost. Paul tells us not to be ignorant concerning the Holy Ghost because he is part of the Godhead. God the Father and God the Son acknowledge the Holy Ghost and their personality as being equal. In St. Matthew 28:19, it reads, *Go ye therefore, and teach all nations, baptizing them in the name of the Father, and of the Son, and of the Holy Ghost.* The benediction ends in 2 Corinthians 13:14, *The grace of the Lord Jesus Christ, and the love of God, and the communion of the Holy Ghost be with you all. Amen.*

The Holy Ghost is a witness of Jesus and was sent to take the place of Christ when he went back to heaven. St. John 14:16 reads, *And I will pray the Father, and he shall give you another Comforter, that he may abide with you forever.* The disciples felt the presence of God when they received the Holy Ghost. It was just as if Jesus was standing before them. The Holy Ghost is waiting to seal you until the day of promise if you accept Jesus as your personal savior. The Holy Ghost is your last chance. God shows himself to you over and over again. Please do not take these warnings lightly. Do something about your soul and receive God in your heart at this moment. The Holy Ghost confirms everything the Father and Son have told you in the past. The message is the same as it was from past times. God does not change. Remember the Holy Ghost is a part of the

Godhead. He possesses the same qualities as the Father and Son. Many people grieve the Holy Ghost by wasting time and playing with their souls day after day. The end of the world is closer now than it was ever before and taking a chance is the wrong thing to do.

The Bible speaks of the Holy Ghost as coming to bring joy and give us a pure heart with victory over the enemy. All we have to do is listen to and obey the spirit. The Holy Ghost is ready to speak many great things through you. He also wants to bring you blessings, healing, and miracles. This is why it is important to be an effective witness for God. The Holy Ghost wants to move in you so others will be attracted to the fire they see burning in you. Yes, the Holy Ghost beings love, peace, and joy. He is no different from God the Father, and Son. Today can be your day. The Holy Ghost moves across the world and is ready for you to accept him into you heart.

THIS BOOK DOES NOT HAVE TO BE ABOUT YOU
LET JESUS IN

CHAPTER 11 NOTES

THE HOLY GHOST

EXPLAIN

_____

_____

_____

_____

_____

_____

_____

_____

_____

_____

_____

_____

_____

_____

_____

EPILOUGE

GOD THE FATHER

The Bible says that no man knows the end of time, except God the Father. God is going to tell his son Jesus "It is done." Jesus is going to come back on a cloud in a twinkle of an eye, at his Father's command. He will come to take his church home. God is going to call the Holy Ghost back to Heaven as well. God's wrath will be loose upon the earth. The entire world will be judged. Make sure you have made your soul right with God. Jesus is standing at you heart's door knocking. Simply, "Let Him In."